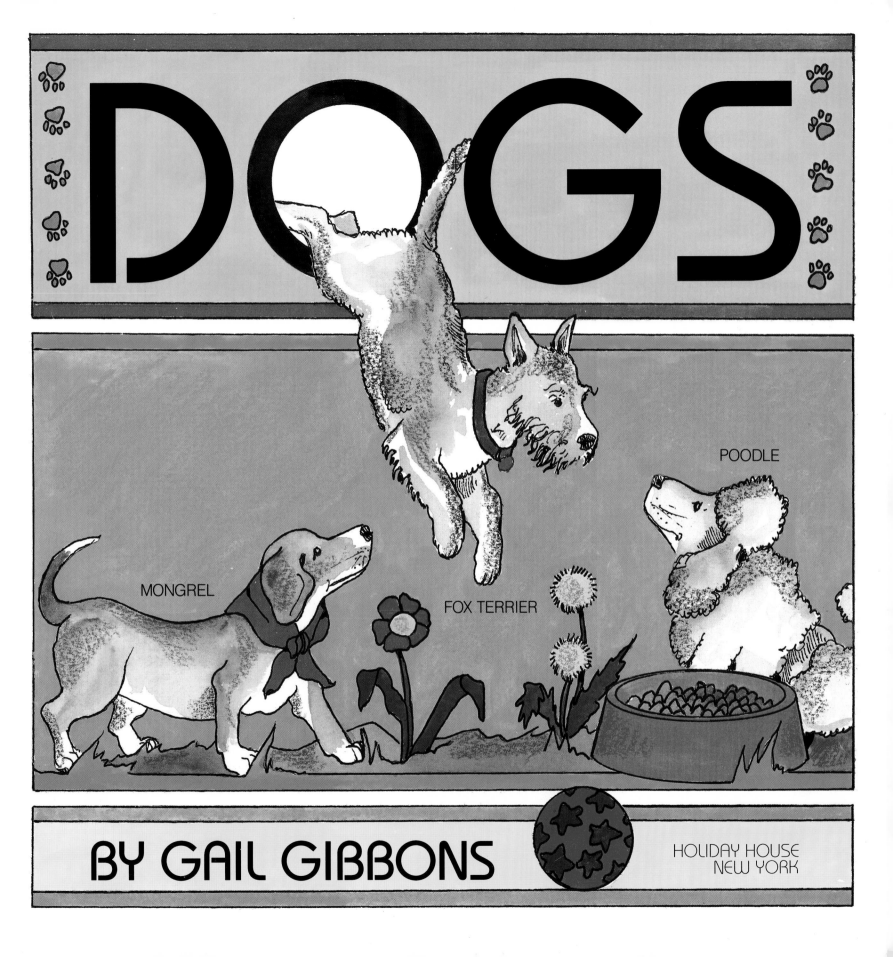

DOGS

MONGREL

FOX TERRIER

POODLE

BY GAIL GIBBONS

HOLIDAY HOUSE
NEW YORK

TO WILTON
ALSO TO GRACE AND HER MOFFAT & SHEENA

SPECIAL THANKS TO
DANIEL J. KELLY, D.V.M of
STONECLIFF ANIMAL CLINIC,
BRADFORD, VERMONT

Copyright © 1996 by Gail Gibbons
All rights reserved
Printed in the United States of America
Library of Congress Cataloging-in-Publication Data
Gibbons, Gail.
Dogs / Gail Gibbons. — 1st ed.
p.   cm.
Summary: An introduction to dogs including their history,
types of breeds, senses, and ways of communication.
ISBN 0-8234-1226-1 (hardcover : alk. paper)
1. Dogs—Juvenile literature.   [1. Dogs.]   I. Title.
SF426.5.G53   1996   95-24966   CIP   AC
636.7—dc20

ISBN 0-8234-1335-7 (pbk.)

ISBN-13: 978-0-8234-1226-6 (hardcover)
ISBN-13: 978-0-8234-1335-5 (pbk)

ISBN-10: 0-8234-1226-1 (hardcover)
ISBN-10: 0-8234-1335-7 (pbk)

A dog can be a good pet. It can play with a ball, romp along-side a bicycle, go for a ride in a car or just be a loyal friend.

The first ancestors of wolves and dogs lived over 50 million years ago. Over time these creatures developed into wolves. All dogs are descendents of wolves.

Wolves and dogs are members of the dog family called Canidae. Both are social animals. Wolves live in groups called packs.

About 15,000 years ago tamed dogs began to live with people and became pets.

GOLDEN RETRIEVERS

These are PUREBRED dogs.

Over time these tame dogs began to look different from wolves. Today there are different kinds of dogs called breeds. The pure-bred is a dog whose father and mother belong to the same breed.

CROSSBREED

MONGRELS
or
MUTTS

GERMAN SHEPHERD and
ROTTWEILER MIX

A dog whose parents belong to two different breeds is called a crossbreed. A mongrel is a mix of many different kinds of dogs. All of these dogs make good pets.

SAINT BERNARD

GREYHOUND

DACHSHUND

CHIHUAHUA

Some dogs have short legs, others have long legs. Some dogs are very small. Others can be very large.

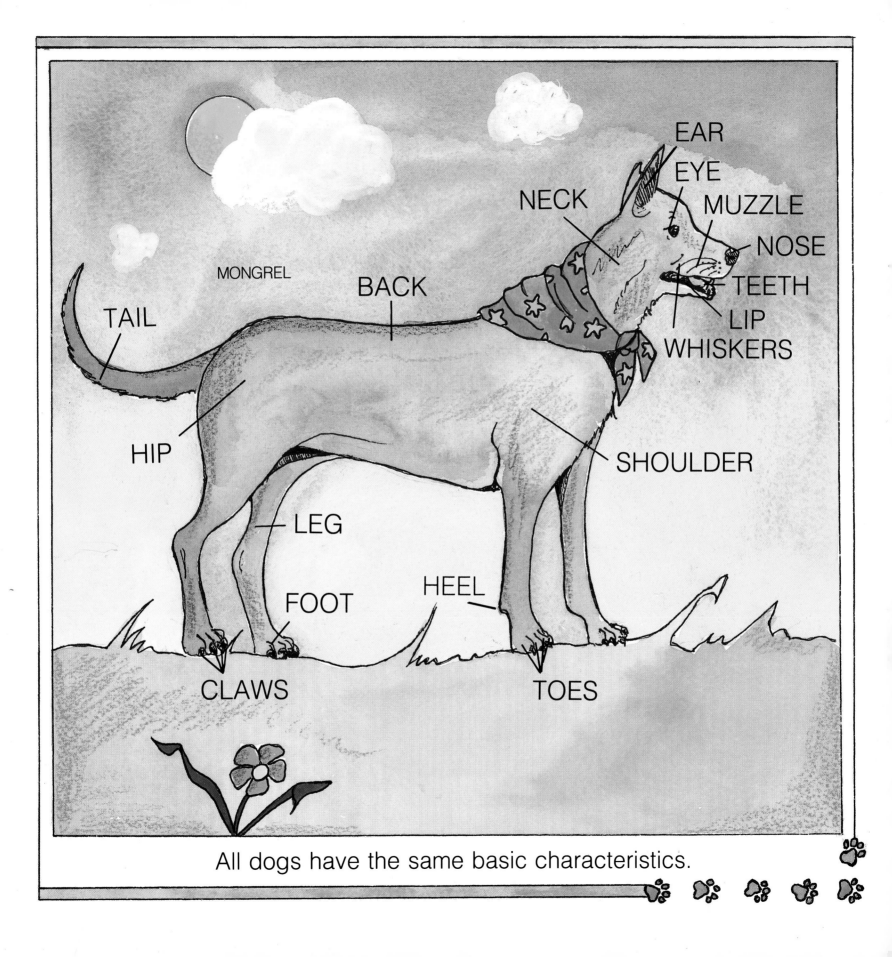

EAR
EYE
MUZZLE
NOSE
NECK
TEETH
LIP
WHISKERS
MONGREL
BACK
TAIL
HIP
SHOULDER
LEG
HEEL
FOOT
CLAWS
TOES

All dogs have the same basic characteristics.

CANINE TEETH or FANGS

MONGREL

DOG

Dogs have forty-two teeth for tearing, chewing and grinding their food. Four of their teeth are called canine teeth, or fangs.

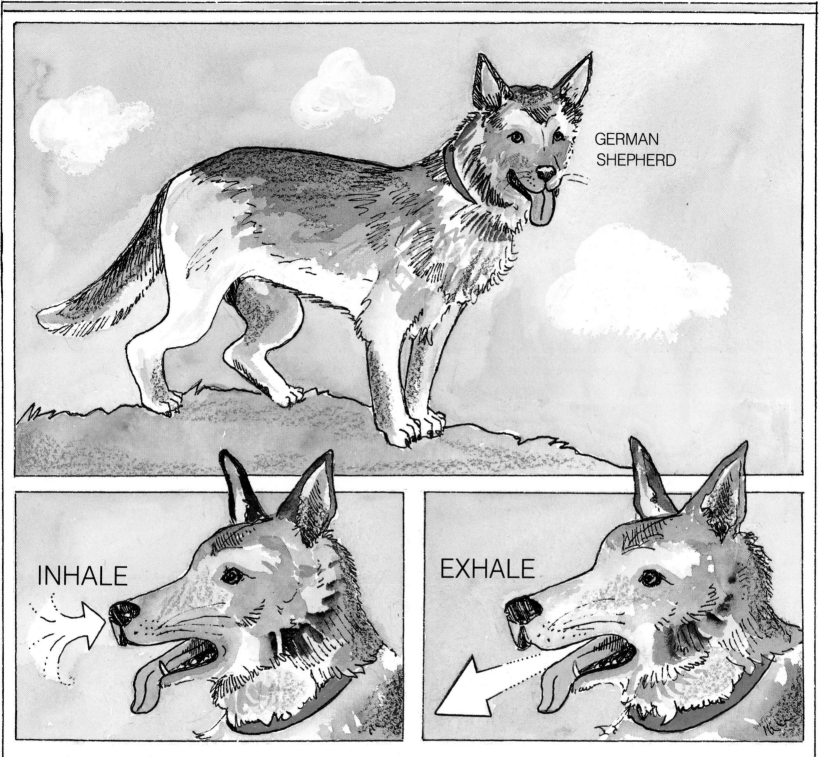

Dogs pant to stay cool. They don't sweat. When a dog inhales it breathes in fresh air through its cool wet nose. Then it exhales the body's heat through its mouth.

Sniff . . . sniff . . . Smell is a dog's sharpest sense. Inside the nose are about 300 million cells that help identify odors. A person has about 50 million of these cells. That's why dogs have a better sense of smell than people. A dog can even smell an old bone that's buried two feet in the dirt.

Dogs have a keen sense of hearing, too. If a dog raises its ears, it is listening to sounds. Often they are sounds people can't hear. That is because dogs can hear four times better than people.

Dogs can't see better than people. In fact, some scientists think dogs see in shades of gray. But they do have better night vision than people. They can spot the smallest movement at a distance in the dark.

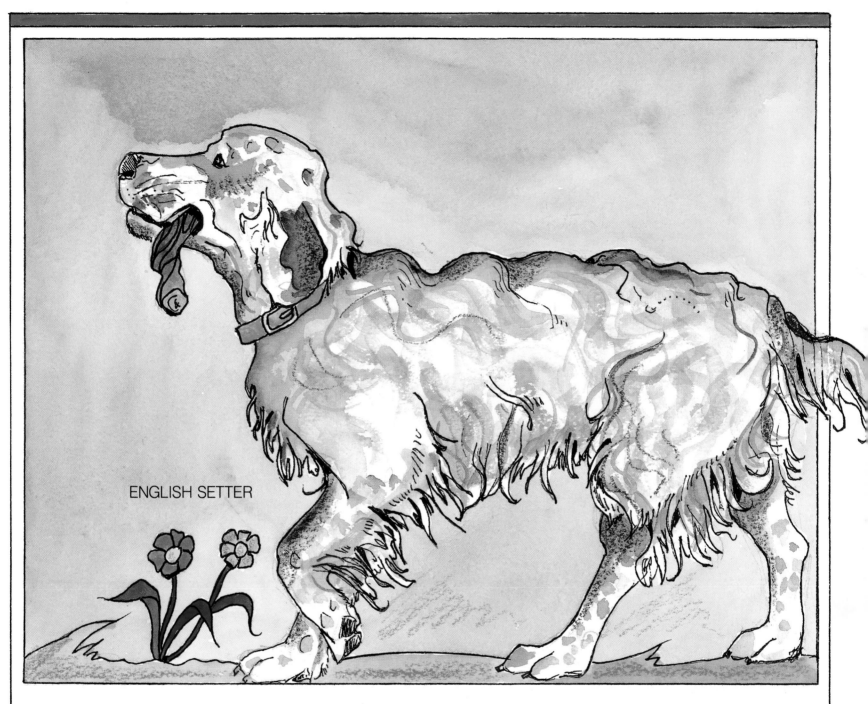

ENGLISH SETTER

Most dogs have two coats of fur. The outer fur, called the guard fur, protects a dog against rain or snow. The inner fur, called the undercoat, keeps the dog warm.

A dog gets some of its sense of touch with its whiskers. The whiskers are connected to many nerves.

The CLAWS are used for gripping the ground and for digging.

The PADS on a dog's paws act as a cushion.

TOES

HEEL

PAW

GREYHOUND

Dogs don't stand, walk or run using their entire foot like people do. Instead they stand on their toes, called paws. The heels of their feet are high up on their legs. Because of this, dogs can run quickly. The fastest dog, a Greyhound, can run about forty miles an hour!

Dogs have ways of communicating or "talking" when they meet. They stand tall with their tails up and try to stare each other down. They are deciding who is top dog, or leader. If one rolls over, it is saying to the other "You're top dog."

Dogs communicate in other ways, too. A happy dog wags its tail. An angry dog sometimes bares its teeth. A scared dog holds its tail between its legs, and its ears may go flat against its head.

Dogs make different sounds to communicate, too. A scared, restless or excited dog whines. A woof may be a warning. An angry dog can growl and bark. Sometimes a playful dog barks.

The father is called a SIRE.

NEWFOUNDLAND

The mother is called a DAM.

LITTER

PUPPY

A baby dog is called a puppy. The mother dog usually gives birth to one to twelve puppies in a group called a litter. She nurses them.

Their eyes and ears open in about two weeks. When they are about three weeks old they begin to eat solid foods. The puppies now play with each other. They are cute and cuddly.

Between four and ten weeks of age, puppies spend most of their time playing and exploring. Most likely a puppy will become a good pet if it is around people at this time. It is learning to be a social animal.

The best time to adopt a puppy is when it is about eight to ten weeks old. It is old enough to leave its mother. Sometimes people adopt older dogs that don't have a home and need one.

HOW TO CARE FOR A PUPPY

When you bring a puppy home, keep it in a confined space. Do not let it roam. This helps a puppy feel secure. Handle it gently and speak softly.

Feed the puppy about four times a day. Food for puppies should be different than food for grown dogs.

Patiently teach your puppy to go to the bathroom outside. Then the puppy is housebroken.

Your puppy should have fresh water available at all times.

Keep your puppy clean.

Make sure your puppy has safe toys to play with. All puppies need exercise.

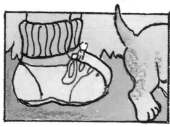

Don't leave your puppy outside unattended.

Begin leash training your puppy.

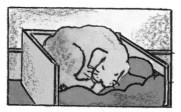

Make your puppy a nice, cozy bed to sleep in.

Take your puppy to the veterinarian for its checkup and its puppy shots.

Most of all, your puppy needs you. Love your puppy!

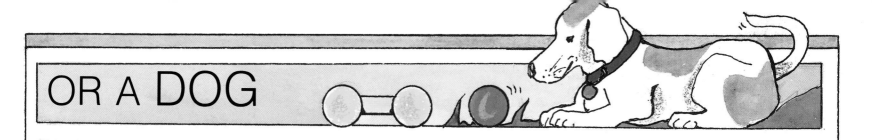

Feed your dog one or two times a day on a regular schedule. Ask your veterinarian for advice.

Your dog should have safe toys.

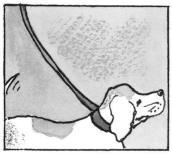

Walk your dog at scheduled times each day for exercise, and so it can go to the bathroom.

Your dog should have a nice, cozy bed to sleep in.

Your dog should have fresh water available at all times.

Take your dog to the veterinarian for its yearly checkup and shots. If your dog looks sick or injured, bring it to a vet.

Keep your dog clean and groomed.

Remember . . . a dog needs love and care just like you do.

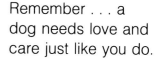

Besides being good friends, dogs help people in many ways. Many blind people depend on the eyes of their guide dogs to see for them. Some dogs help farmers round up sheep in the countryside.

Sometimes dog teams pull heavy snow sleds. Police dogs are trained to help solve crimes. Some people have a pet dog to guard the family home.

SCOTTISH
TERRIER

Sometimes people enter dogs in dog shows. "Best Dog in the Show" is the champion! In the United States there are about 2000 dog shows a year.

Best of all, dogs are wonderful pets, big or small, purebred or mongrel. They can be loyal and good friends.

PAW PRINTS

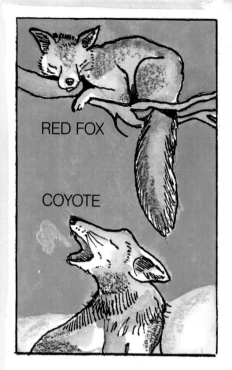

RED FOX

COYOTE

There are about 35 different kinds of wild dogs such as the gray wolf, the red fox, the coyote and others.

WOLF-HOUND

GREAT DANE

The tallest dogs of all are the Wolfhound and the Great Dane. They measure over three feet tall at their shoulders.

CORGI

Scientists say people feel better when they have dogs as companions or can simply pet them. A person's blood pressure may drop, which is good for one's health.

CHIHUAHUA

The smallest dog of all is the miniature Chihuahua. It is no bigger than a tea cup and can weigh as little as one pound.

COLLIE

Most of a dog's growing up is done in the first two years of its life.

SAINT BERNARD

The heaviest dog is the Saint Bernard. One actually weighed over 300 pounds!

OLD ENGLISH SHEEPDOG

DACHSHUND

A small or medium size dog may live to be about 15 years old. A big dog may live to be about 10 years old.

ANIMA

In many places there are humane societies, also called animal shelters, that help stray and un-wanted dogs. They take care of lost and sick dogs that have no homes. A person can go there to adopt one.

FAMOUS DOGS

Sater was the only one of 50 watch-dogs in ancient Greece that survived an attack by invaders. It ran to the gates of its town to warn the citizens.

About 150 years ago there lived a famous Saint Bernard named Barry that rescued many people trapped in snow.

About 1000 years ago, the king of Norway put a dog named Saur on the throne and demanded that it be treated like royalty.

Laika was the first dog to travel in space. Laika was aboard the Russian satellite, *Sputnik II,* in 1957.

LASSIE   BEETHOVEN   RIN-TIN-TIN

Some dogs are movie stars such as Rin-Tin-Tin, Lassie, and Beethoven.